P9-DNQ-010

FROM DRUMS TO HARP

The Story of
Drummer and Harpist
Robert M. Garcia

Vee Williams Garcia

TEMPLE TERRACE PUBLIC LIBRARY
202 Bullard Park Way
Temple Terrace, Fla. 33617

NOV 3 0 2010

iUniverse, Inc.
New York   Bloomington

FROM DRUMS TO HARP
The Story of Drummer and Harpist Robert M. Garcia

Copyright © 2006, 2010 by Vee Williams Garcia

All rights reserved. No part of this book may be used or reproduced by any means, graphic, electronic, or mechanical, including photocopying, recording, taping or by any information storage retrieval system without the written permission of the publisher except in the case of brief quotations embodied in critical articles and reviews.

iUniverse books may be ordered through booksellers or by contacting:

iUniverse
1663 Liberty Drive
Bloomington, IN 47403
www.iuniverse.com
1-800-Authors (1-800-288-4677)

Because of the dynamic nature of the Internet, any Web addresses or links contained in this book may have changed since publication and may no longer be valid. The views expressed in this work are solely those of the author and do not necessarily reflect the views of the publisher, and the publisher hereby disclaims any responsibility for them.

ISBN: 978-1-4502-4464-0 (sc)
ISBN: 978-1-4502-5044-3 (dj)
ISBN: 978-1-4502-4465-7 (ebk)

Printed in the United States of America

iUniverse rev. date: 08/02/2010

FROM DRUMS TO HARP

DEDICATION

To
Robert
Garcia's
family and
friends, plus his
fellow musicians
and the many others
who loved him and admired
his masterful playing of the
drums and his versatile playing
of the grand harp.

Contents

ACKNOWLEDGMENTS

I am grateful to Ellen Williams, Robert Garcia's mother, for providing me with early photographs of Robert along with his early biographical information, from which I selected material for use in this book.

I thank the jazz singers and musicians in Tampa-St. Petersburg, Clearwater, Lakeland, and elsewhere in the Tampa Bay area; as well as in Tallahassee, Gainesville, and other areas of Florida. My thanks also to those musicians based in Memphis, Tennessee; Denver, Colorado; and other cities at press time who shared with me their thoughts about Robert Garcia the man and Robert Garcia the musician. Their comments, some of which are quoted on the following pages, have helped to make this book a treasure.

Finally, I thank my sister and editor, Dorothy C. Colding of Hyattsville, Maryland, for her invaluable expertise. With her years of professional experience and deep insight, Dottie inspired and encouraged me as I worked on this wonderful project.

AUTHOR'S FOREWARD

My purpose for writing this book was not to produce a full-fledged biography, but rather to provide the highlights of Drummer and Harpist Robert M. Garcia's life and music career. In keeping with my purpose, I focused on three areas: (1) his amazing musical talent and accomplishments, including switching from drums to harp as his instrument of choice late in his career; (2) his spiritual legacy, which was a combination of positive energy, good values, and love; and (3) his concrete legacy.

It was my privilege and pleasure as Robert Garcia's wife to witness and experience his masterful and versatile playing of the xylophone, the vibraphone, the conga drums, the drum set, and the grand harp in our home and in myriad public venues.

It was a blessing for me to develop a greater love of music as a direct result of being Robert's wife. Just as his selfless giving as a man ensured that our marriage was a good one, his talent and giving as a musician positively impacted my life. Robert helped to enhance my appreciation and love of the music; which I was first exposed to many years before I met him. I am referring to the music on my parents' long playing records by Louis Armstrong,

Ella Fitzgerald, Sarah Vaughan, and Duke Ellington, and other jazz legends that I heard as a child; and the televised and live performances of classic and contemporary jazz singers and instrumentalists that I witnessed after I became an adult. Robert helped me to become a better listener. After I heard him and his fellow musicians play in trios, quartets, bands, and orchestras often and in many venues, I learned to distinguish the sounds of different instruments from their blend, with little effort. I also learned to appreciate the combinations of various instruments that Robert sometimes put together—combinations that, as far as I knew, I had never heard before.

My husband also inspired me to become more active and successful with my writing. When I met Robert in the fall of 1990, I was writing and publishing poems. He was very supportive of my poetry, giving me time and space in which to write. After we were married, in October 1991, he helped me to set up a separate room in our home to use as my writing room, and he made sure I had the equipment I needed to operate effectively. Additionally, on many occasions he played harp music to accompany my public poetry readings.

A few years after we were married, I began writing my first novel. A couple of years later, I finished the novel, and Robert helped me to seek and find a publisher for it. After my novel was published in 2000, he even accompanied me during my tour to promote the book. I believe that the energy he infused in me, while simultaneously pursuing his music career, was what fueled me to begin writing my second novel.

An amazing energy radiated from Robert, and it seemed to warm and energize everyone in his presence. Robert had a broad smile and hearty laughter. He saw the positive side of every situation and always looked for the good in people. Robert believed in showing love and respect for all people—regardless of race, color, or creed—and in treating them the way he wanted to be treated. His spiritual goodness manifested itself in his talk and in his walk.

Unfortunately, Robert's untimely passing from this world prevented him from leaving a tangible legacy, at least the CD he had planned to produce and put on the market. Therefore I offer this book, humbly and respectfully, hoping it will somehow serve in its stead.

Vee Williams Garcia
Washington, DC
June 2010

INTRODUCTION

Robert M. Garcia, a musician of African American and Cuban descent, seemed chosen by the Creator to become a special person and a musical genius. As a young child, Robert had the rhythm of a much older person. Before he started elementary school, he received a drum for Christmas. His prodigious drumming started with that first instrument.

Although he was full of vitality, Robert had a gentle spirit. He was quiet and shy when he was a little boy. During his teenage years, he was still rather quiet. But later, after he became a young adult, he began to develop a hearty personality, which was reflected in his bright smile and robust laughter. Robert's laughter started deep down inside him, traveled up and out into the air, and shook his entire body. He made everyone around him feel good when he laughed. Always outgoing with a ready smile, Robert loved people and loved to socialize. Those qualities served him well as he grew from young adulthood towards his more mature years.

Robert studied musical instruments and played in orchestras, bands and ensembles while he was in junior high, high school, and college. He became a professional drummer while he was a teenager, and he used his musical genius later in life to bring happiness to people in all walks of life.

As an adult, Garcia taught music and provided many young students and adult musicians with opportunities to play music professionally. He lived a life filled with studying and playing music. During his lifetime he played the clarinet, trumpet, snare drum, tympani, the traditional drum set, conga drums, the xylophone, vibraphone, and the grand harp. He was a major talent on the drums and became widely known as a master drummer.

Because Robert played drums passionately for so many years, people were surprised when he shifted his focus from drums to the grand harp. Especially since the two instruments are very different from each other. Why would a percussionist, such a marvelous drummer, choose strings and the grand harp of all things, as his next instrument to play professionally? To Garcia the radical change was logical. His reasons for the great switch can be found on the pages of this book.

The kinds of music he played on the harp included classical, sacred, pop, R&B, funk, new age, blues, and jazz. Robert loved music and he adored the grand harp. When he played for audiences, his music entertained, inspired, instructed, soothed, and occasionally even shocked some listeners. Many people were surprised to learn that the harp could be such a versatile instrument. But then Robert was a versatile musician.

He played a wide variety of music on the harp, not only as a soloist, but also in various ensembles. His versatility was outstanding and innovative as it amazed harp instructors and classical harpists, as well as other instrumentalists. Robert Garcia, a musical genius of the South, was a musician for all people and for all seasons.

BEGINNINGS

Childhood photo of Robert Garcia

Robert Michael Garcia was born in Tampa, Florida, on August 18, 1950. As early as age three, Robert showed he had the rhythm of a much older person. He danced around the house and drummed on furniture and anything else that would withstand the forceful energy of his little hands. Before he started elementary school, he received a drum for Christmas. And his prodigious drumming began with that first instrument.

While Robert Garcia was a young child, he lived with his mother, Ellen Williams and her family on 9th Avenue, in Tampa's Ybor City, an area which at the time was inhabited largely by African Americans and Cubans. During his elementary age years, he attended St. Peter Claver Catholic School and Potter Elementary School, in Tampa.

Later on, young Robert lived on 20th Street, in Ybor City, in another loving and supportive environment with his father, Rigoberto Garcia, and his grandparents, Juan and Cassie Garcia.

A childhood and life-long friend of Robert's, named Albert "Chico" Arenas, has good memories of that time. The following is a special memory clip from a time that Chico says was full for both of them and their families:

Bobby's dad, Rigoberto, played semi-pro baseball with my dad. His uncles, Sam and William, also played baseball on those teams. So imagine Robert, his family, with his dad and uncles playing, and my family with my dad playing and managing on the same team—all happening on Sundays, after church, around noon.

During the early to mid-1960s, Robert Garcia attended Charles Young Jr. High School. At Charles Young, he learned to play both the clarinet and trumpet and was in the school band. He also played the snare drum and the timpani during his junior high years.

In high school, Garcia became very popular as a drummer in the Middleton High School Band. His membership in the band and his good relationships with his classmates and other friends at Middleton were sources of pride for him. Robert valued his fellow band members and other friends at Middleton. He continued to nourish those relationships long after high school.

While Robert was a teenager, he gained two brothers, Rigo Garcia and Renaldo Garcia. Robert loved his brothers, and through the years he shared many meaningful and enjoyable times with them.

After graduating from Middleton High School in the Class of 1968, Robert spent much of the summer playing drums in bands in Tampa-St. Petersburg and elsewhere in the Tampa Bay area. Like most jazz musicians, he had learned much and become a better drummer by playing in bands and jam sessions. Robert had studied technique and theory with a few European art music teachers in Tampa. But he had outgrown those teachers, especially with regard to jazz music. He began going to concerts and watching professional jazz drummers from other cities perform new and outstanding techniques. He wanted to learn those new techniques.

It was during the late 1960s that jazz education was introduced into universities and colleges. In the autumn of 1968, Robert matriculated at Florida A & M University (FAMU), in Tallahassee, Florida, where he majored in music. He became a member of both the FAMU Jazz Band and the FAMU Percussion Ensemble for two years.

At FAMU, Garcia also joined the drum line of the world famous FAMU Marching 100 Band. A fellow Marching 100 band member named Whitman Able, who at the time played clarinet, remembers the following incident that in retrospect sounds amusing to him, but which did not seem amusing to him or Robert at the time.

During our sophomore year at FAMU and as Marching 100 Band members, Robert and I foolishly followed a long time band tradition and would haze freshmen band members.

Well, one of those freshman band members blew the whistle on us, and that resulted in our suspension from the band for hazing. That really hurt. My mother got the letter and chewed me out. After that incident, Robert and I got out of touch somehow, and the next thing I heard was that he was attending Berklee College of Music.

Robert entered the Berklee College of Music on a full scholarship during the summer of 1970. While there, he lived in the school's dormitory. He was proud to be a student at Berklee, majoring in Composition. He wanted to use his experience there to become an even better jazz musician.

Robert told his mother, and many years later he related to his wife, that at Berklee he was offered a job – a job to teach a class! Neither his mother nor his wife doubted it, because Robert was a gifted drummer and had grown up playing jazz. He had been a professional jazz drummer before entering Berklee, and before jazz education programs were introduced into universities and colleges in the late 1960s.

At Berklee, Robert was very happy for a while. Among his classes were Percussion, Harmony, Melody and Improvisation, Piano Functional, Jazz History, Ear Training, Ensemble, Workshop, and Arranging.

He studied at Berklee for three semesters: Summer 1970, Fall 1970, and Spring 1971. He did exceptionally well during his first two semesters. However, before the Spring Semester started, he had begun to miss his family, friends, and other close Florida support systems. The shock of a different culture, plus the very cold winter weather in Boston did not help to ease his loneliness.

He missed Florida so much that he became extremely unhappy. He was essentially alone and lonely in Boston. As a result his grades began to decline. Unfortunately, in those days Berklee did not have counselors to help students who might have had difficulty adjusting to a place so different from their hometown environment. On a few occasions, Robert telephoned his uncle, William Woods, who was in his late twenties at the time, and asked him to come to Boston to live for a while.

As much as he loved Robert, however, William had his own personal reasons for not being able to travel that long distance, over 1,000 miles from Florida, all the way to Massachusetts. He told Robert he could not come. And Robert, still feeling very unhappy about the idea of remaining that far from home, alone, struggled over whether he should stay, or whether he should leave Berklee.

He decided to tough it out for a while longer; which enabled him to complete the Spring 1971 semester. He registered for the Fall 1971 semester, and a fall class schedule was made for him. But ultimately he decided not to remain at Berklee, after all. Instead he returned home to Florida in May 1971.

Once Robert was back in Tampa, the city's warm climate and the gentle breezes from the Gulf of Mexico embraced him. Palm trees, majestic oaks, mango and orange trees; and familiar tropical birds and flowers welcomed him. He settled down and, surrounded finally by close family, friends and associates in the Sunshine State continued his life as a professional musician.

A SPECIAL DRUMMER

Robert had so much finesse with the drums, and yet he played with so much power!

---- Vincent Sims,
Guitarist

A SPECIAL DRUMMER

Robert, who was called Bobby by some of his friends and associates and simply Garcia by others, played drums professionally for years in Tampa, Clearwater, and St. Petersburg, Florida, as well as in many other cities around the Tampa Bay area. He later ventured away from the Bay area to perform in more distant cities such as Orlando, Daytona, Gainesville, Jacksonville, Tallahassee, and West Palm Beach. He also played drums in Miami and other cities in southern Florida. He played at VFW clubs, various commercial nightclubs, at churches, synagogues, and other indoor and outdoor venues where he was asked to play. There were times when he volunteered his services. But most of the time he worked for payment. After all, he had been a professional musician since he was seventeen years old.

In addition to playing drums professionally, Garcia also played the vibraphone. Eventually he played both instruments not only in the Bay area but all around Florida, as well as in Washington, DC; Newport News, Virginia; St. Louis, Missouri; New Mexico and elsewhere. He became well known as a drummer and supported himself as a musician for many years.

Robert Garcia had the pleasure and honor of playing with such international jazz giants as trumpeter and cornet player Nat Adderley, who was a personal friend of his; drummer Max Roach; and trumpet player and trombonist Buster Cooper.

During his music career, Garcia's drumming provided the heart beat in bands that included such Florida, and nationally and internationally known greats as pianist and band leader Al Downing; keyboardist-writer-arranger Quency Jennings (formerly of K.C. & The Sunshine Band; keyboardists Ladyfingers (a.k.a. Normita R. Jeffery), and Kevin Wilder; vibraphonist and keyboardist Ricky Lyons; drummers Greg Williams, Henry Page, and Ron Gregg; drummer and vocalist Turk Nelson, bass players Steve Cooper, William "B" Bennett, Ed Lanier, and Michael Ross; guitarist and bassist Kenny Walker; guitarists Vincent Sims and Charlie Robinson; trumpet players Marcus Hampton and Shaheed Darby; saxophonists Henry Ashwood and Ernie Calhoun; trombonist Albert "Chico" Arenas; singer and flutist Ronda Paramoure; and flutist Linda Nash; pop and R&B singer Dori Freeman; also gospel/inspirational and jazz singers Rosalyn Vasquez and Belinda Womack; and jazz vocalists Rose Bilal, Theo Valentine, and Darele Campbell.

Although Robert was chiefly an instrumentalist, he sometimes exhibited his ability as a vocalist. In Florida, he occasionally sang at programs for the public. Sometimes he sang in church, and other times in secular venues. His singing voice was deep and rich, and when he sang people appeared to be a little shocked to see him, a percussionist and player of other instruments, break into song. However, their shocked expressions soon changed to that of pleasant surprise.

In addition to his ability in the performing arts, Robert's creative talent also manifested itself in the visual arts. During his young adult years and well into his thirties until he was around forty, he spent some of his time painting colorful artwork. Using oils and acrylics, he painted portraits and still life images on canvas. From the mid-1970s until 1990 or so, this special drummer and sometime singer was also a member of the Tampa Bay area visual arts community.

Eventually Garcia began to spend less time painting, but he continued to support his associates in the visual arts community by attending their shows and exhibits, and by occasionally helping them to mount their exhibits or set up for receptions that followed their exhibits. However, Robert's interest in the visual arts could not compete with his love for the performing arts, especially his playing of instruments such as the xylophone, vibraphone, congas, and the drum set. And he was indeed a gifted drummer.

FROM DRUMS TO HARP

Robert was versatile. He went from drums to harp.
He saw areas in music that hadn't been explored by
other musicians, and he explored them to the max.

---- Henry Ashwood
Saxophonist

I respected Robert when he changed from drums to
harp. It's not easy to do that. They're totally different
instruments. But he stuck with it 'til he got it. And
he kept it going.

---- William "B" Bennett
Bassist

FROM DRUMS TO HARP

In the mid-to-late 1980s, Robert purchased a student harp and later benefited from studying with Kathryn Holm, a harp instructor at the University of South Florida at the time. When not in class he used to practice in a music room in the Fine Arts Department of USF. And he would sometimes practice off campus with professional base players he knew in Tampa and  St. Petersburg, Florida. Garcia was still studying and practicing at the University when he met a young lady who would become important to him for the rest of his life.

In October 1990 Robert met Virginia Williams, a poet and writer who had relocated from Washington, DC, to Tampa in April of the same year. On a mild evening in late October, the two met at a visual arts exhibit and reception, at the Orange Blossom Room, a well-known public events hall in Tampa. A mutual friend and patron of the arts, Wanda Mundy, introduced them. Virginia and Wanda had come to the exhibit together. When the event was almost over, Wanda and Virginia, ready to leave, were walking through the kitchen and towards the door leading to the parking lot. Robert was in the kitchen, at the sink, washing a few pans and otherwise helping the art exhibit's reception committee to clean up the room. Wanda spotted Robert, spoke to him and casually introduced him to Virginia. Wanda then proceeded to the parking lot to retrieve her car, allowing Robert and Virginia to chat alone for a few moments. During their conversation, Robert asked Virginia for her phone number. The ease and trust she felt in his presence caused her to write the number on a slip of paper from her purse and give it to him. Robert dried his hands quickly and accepted the slip of paper with a smile. He tucked it in his wallet and promised to call her.

A few weeks later, Robert telephoned Virginia. After becoming more acquainted with each other via several phone conversations, the pair began dating. By then it was late November, and on a few balmy nights they took strolls together along the tree-lined streets of Tampa's chic Hyde Park neighborhood. In the spirit of Christmas, the area's tree tops, lamp posts, and its unique shops and outdoor cafes were brightly lit with tiny sparkling white lights and colorful Yuletide decorations.

On some of their dates, Robert and Virginia would go to dinner and a movie in Hyde Park or in one of the other neighborhoods of Tampa. The couple also went on long drives together, along Tampa's scenic and elegant Bayshore Boulevard, and around the city of Tampa; along Clearwater Beach and Sand Key, and sometimes to St. Petersburg Beach. In addition to affording them romantic times together, during which they came to know more and more about each other, their drives enabled Virginia to see and learn much about the beautiful Tampa Bay area that she had not seen or known about before.

After Robert felt bonded to Virginia, he began introducing her to his friends, two of whom invited them for Thanksgiving dinner. Robert and Virginia accepted. They enjoyed the sumptuous Thanksgiving Day meal, as well as the music and the conversation they shared with Robert's friends and their holiday guests.

Soon, Virginia learned how important family was to Robert. On Christmas Eve, after they arrived for dinner at his father's home in the Carrollwood neighborhood of Tampa, Robert introduced Virginia to his father, Rigoberto Garcia and his father's wife, Sonja Garcia. He then introduced her to his brothers, Rigo and Renaldo Garcia, and to his Cuban, Afro Cuban, and American aunts, uncles, and cousins from his father's family. Many relatives and friends of the family were there, and everyone made Virginia feel at home.

Robert and Virginia spent Christmas Day with Robert's mother, Ellen Williams and her family. They all gathered together and spent the day at the home of Robert's aunt and uncle Bebe and Floyd Garrett, in Temple Terrace, a quiet neighborhood in the Northeast area of Tampa. Ellen and her family welcomed Virginia. Throughout the early afternoon and on through the evening, the wonderful sounds of Christmas music floated from the stereo, and Christmas Day parades and football games were on the large screen TV. Robert's Aunt Bebe and her daughters, Carmen, Linda, and Maria, served a wonderful home cooked Christmas Day meal. Virginia felt very comfortable among Robert's maternal aunts, uncles, and cousins.

The fact that Robert wanted to be with Virginia on major national holidays impressed Virginia. She was impressed; because many of the single women she knew in DC and in Tampa complained that the men they dated and really liked always disappeared around the holidays. They would reappear sometime in January, after New Year's Day was over. The fact that Robert exposed Virginia to his family and friends so early in their relationship and was with her at Christmas Time, New Year's Day and subsequent major holidays during the New Year was very assuring, very gratifying for her. She was sure it was a sign that Robert was serious about her and wanted to keep her in his life.

*** *** ***

After spending time with both sides of Robert's family during that Christmas of 1990, the couple continued dating. Virginia went with Robert to a gig he played on New Year's Eve. On New Year's Day, they attended an all day barbecue and music fest in the spacious grassy yard surrounding Bassist Steve Cooper's ranch style home in St. Petersburg. Many Bay area musicians and their significant others were there. Between jam sessions, the musicians joined their wives and girlfriends in eating ribs, burgers, hot dogs, corn on the cob, greens, potato salad and green beans. Later they enjoyed their choice of various desserts. The weather was mild and partially sunny. The open air was welcoming and the soft breezes were enveloping, as the jazz musicians and their wives and friends socialized all day long and into the night on that wonderful New Year's Day of 1991.

In addition to that February being Black History Month, the month also marked two important events in the lives of Virginia and Robert. One was Valentine's Day, and the other was Virginia's birthday. Robert was on top of both events, showering Virginia with gifts on both occasions. On Virginia's birthday, Robert told her, "If we're still together in May, I'm going to give you an engagement ring." Virginia remembers feeling very happy, and at the same time she was calm upon hearing Robert say that. To her it would be a natural progression, given the smooth way their relationship had been going.

The months of March and April came and went. As usual, Robert was playing music. At that time, he was the drummer for a jazz and R&B band that played for a talented Bay area singer named Dori Freeman. That gig was a steady Thursday through Saturday night engagement at a classy nightclub called The Fox, which was at that time located in the Westshore area of Tampa. Along with that steady gig and the band rehearsals required for it, Robert managed to squeeze in a couple of weddings and other one-day events as well. Virginia went to The Fox often to see Robert perform. With all of those occasions, March and April of 1991 went by quickly.

In May, as he had promised, Robert presented Virginia with an engagement ring. Virginia was ecstatic about their engagement and so was Robert. Neither of them had doubts. They knew they were doing the right thing. They set their wedding date for October 5th.

The summer came and flew by. Robert and Virginia had so much to do. They had to attend a number of advisory sessions at the home of their pastor, Louis Jones. Virginia had to select and order wedding invitations. She needed to go shopping for a wedding gown. The couple had to be sure to drive downtown and get their marriage license. Also they were feverishly looking for a house in which they would live together.

Robert and Virginia finally found a house that suited them, and they moved into it at the end of August. During September, they completed furnishing and decorating the house. On October 2nd, three days before the wedding, Virginia's out of town relatives and friends began arriving in town. It was a very exciting time.

On Saturday, October 5, 1991, Robert and Virginia were married by Rev. Louis Jones, in a well-attended ceremony at River Grove United Methodist Church, on Sligh Avenue, near 43rd Street, in Tampa. It was the second marriage for both. A reception was held for them in the church social hall following the wedding.

Robert and Virginia posing happily inside River Grove U.M. Church, following their wedding ceremony

After the reception was over, Virginia and Robert and their close family and friends went to the newlyweds' home for an informal gathering. It was a warm, comfortable, and joyous occasion for the newlyweds and their family and friends.

Having arranged for Andrea Hines, one of Virginia's bridesmaids and long time friends, to house sit for them, Robert and Virginia left Tampa for their honeymoon a few days after their wedding. They drove south, away from Tampa, all the way down Highway 41, past Naples, to Fort Myers, and then on to Marco Island. Their hotel on Marco Island was a short walk from the Island's white sand beach, which was sprinkled with cabanas and lined with palm trees and luxury hotels and condominiums. On the Island, Robert and Virginia enjoyed a wonderful week. It was a great start to their married life.

When they returned from their honeymoon, the newlyweds settled into their domestic life. The house they lived in was on Elmore Avenue, in Tampa Heights, not far from Tampa's Ybor City neighborhood. It was a charming, capacious house, with a brief grassy front yard and a long back yard surrounded by high hedges, honeysuckle vines, magnolia trees and night blooming jasmine.

**Robert and Virginia Garcia lived in this house on Elmore Ave.,
in the Tampa Heights neighborhood of Tampa, Florida from
1991 (the year they were married) until the summer of 1994.
Here they welcomed family and entertained friends, many of
whom were singers, musicians, visual artists, and writers.**

Early during his marriage, Robert made a conscious decision
to play drums less and to focus more time on his harp. Playing
drums had often put him in nightclubs, an environment, he said,
that could threaten his marriage. Playing in clubs caused him to
return home at two or three o'clock in the morning, or even later.
And he did not want to keep doing that. "I love being married," he
said, "and I don't want to jeopardize my marriage in any way."

Another thing that influenced Garcia's change from drums to
harp was the comment from an uninformed member of a band

in which he used to play. The band member said Robert did not need to show up for a certain music rehearsal; because, according to the band member, Robert didn't do anything but keep a beat. Apparently that uninformed band member did not realize that the drums are the heart and soul of the band. It is the drummer who drives the other musicians. And Robert Garcia was a very dynamic drummer. Many professional musicians and seasoned music lovers acclaimed him as a master drummer. However, Garcia had reached a point where he wanted to play melodies and harmonies. Therefore he began focusing on the harp.

His six-foot, two inch frame was several inches taller than his student harp (a harp without pedals). But when he sat in a chair and pulled the harp towards his chest and began to play, his height didn't matter.

Robert sometimes practiced with base player Kenny Walker of St. Petersburg. At other times he practiced with William Bennett, a bassist from New York, who was settled in Tampa. Known simply as "B" by many people, William Bennett had practiced with Robert before and after Robert was married, just as Kenny Walker had. When either bassist was available, he welcomed joining Robert for a practice session at Robert's and Virginia's home in the Tampa Heights neighborhood of Tampa. The bassist and the drummer turned harpist would practice for hours. About his and Robert's practice sessions, Bennett said the following.

Yeah, those sessions helped both of us. They helped Robert in his process of learning and becoming more comfortable with the harp. And they allowed me to review some things I already knew.

A MUSICIAN LIVES
HIS NEW DREAM

A MUSICIAN LIVES
HIS NEW DREAM

Around 1992, Robert acquired a pedal harp (also called a grand harp and a concert harp). At a little over 6 feet tall, Robert was about the same height as his pedal harp. And whereas his student harp had about 36 strings, his grand harp had 47. The grand harp was much heavier than the student harp. An average size person might have found it a challenge to lift the grand harp onto a harp dolly or into a case or the back of a station wagon. Robert was a big man, however, and very strong; and he never seemed to mind lifting the grand harp; which he loved to play.

Robert continued studying harp at the University of South Florida for a few more years, and then he felt confident enough to study and practice on his own.

Between Robert practicing on his own and frequently having fellow musicians stop by to rehearse with him in preparation for music engagements, the sound of live music was constantly filling Robert's and Virginia's home. In fact, music filled the couple's lives. Robert performed publicly whenever opportunities arose. And Virginia was often in the audience at the venues where he played.

Robert and Virginia spent the first few years of their marriage in that lovely house in Tampa Heights. Then a change in the neighborhood began to happen. Two times within a year or two, burglars broke into the house and stole one of the couple's TVs, a stereo, and also some of Robert's instruments and expensive sound equipment, leaving Virginia and Robert feeling extremely violated.

Not long after the second break-in, Robert and Virginia began looking for another place to live. They were attracted to a house on Bonito Street, located in a quiet neighborhood in Northeast Tampa. They bought the house and moved in during the summer of 1994. The house had a large front and back yard, and it was surrounded by huge oak trees. On the sidewalk in front of the house, two palm trees stood in the tree box area. The front yard was like a sanctuary for squirrels, birds and butterflies. Cardinals and blue jays alighted on pink and white azalea bushes during February and March. The scent of night-blooming jasmine and orange blossoms surrounded the house most of the year. The house on Bonito Street proved to be a peaceful and perfect environment for Robert and Virginia to share their artistic lives together.

Robert and Virginia purchased this home on Bonito Street, in Tampa, in the summer of 1994. They lived here creatively, always welcoming their family, musicians, writers, and other friends.

Robert continued to do most of his rehearsing at home, and he welcomed other instrumentalists and singers into his home for group rehearsals for performances. Robert was living his new dream. He loved playing the grand harp. And he began to encounter outspoken curiosity about his choice of instruments.

After discovering that Robert switched from drums to the harp and realizing how unusual such a switch was, many people asked Garcia how easy or how difficult the switch had been, and what was involved in such a transition. Today there are people who still wonder how Robert did it. The following professional music instructors have provided answers.

Elnora Oxendine, who is a music instructor and owner of Oxendine's Music Academy, in Hyattsville, Maryland, had the following to say on the subject of a drummer switching from drums to harp:

It would not be difficult for a person already in music; because he or she would transfer the same kind of passion from one instrument to the other.

Regarding the differences between playing the drums and playing the harp, Ms. Oxendine said:

With The drum set you don't read notes. With the harp you must read music harmonies. Also with the harp, your arm movements and your fingers have to be right. You're using all ten fingers when you play harp. Not too many people make that kind of switch since the harp is not in the same kind of family; it is not similar to the drums.

Vern C. Falby, Ph.D., who is a Music Theory professor at the Peabody Conservatory of the Johns Hopkins University, in Baltimore, Maryland, said the following:

From my experience, the greatest challenge in switching to the grand harp from drums would be the introduction of all the elements of pitch in music—melody, harmony, and structural line. Playing the drum set well as an accompaniment to groups of instruments means that you must be in-sync with melodies, chord progressions, and the way the music breathes, but usually a drummer does not have to worry about actually CREATING these. A harpist does.

The fact that Robert was able to move over to the harp is a sign that he always had a pitched-instrument player nestled within his musical gift. It is a great blessing that he was able to express this part of his musical personality later in his career. The fact that he enjoyed such success at this is clearly a testament to the versatility and depth of his musical talent.

Robert Garcia loved playing various genres of music on the harp, including but not limited to: classical, sacred, spirituals, blues, popular, new age, and jazz. If asked he would play *Pachelbel's Canon, the Wedding March, Ave Maria* and many other classical and sacred numbers with as much ease as he rendered hymns and anthems like *Amazing Grace* and *We Shall Overcome.*

He would fulfill requests to play ballads such as *A Ribbon in the Sky, Endless Love, The Shadow of Your Smile* and *My Funny Valentine* as quickly as he would play jazz pieces like *Satin Doll, Killer Joe, Cantaloupe Island,* and *In a Mellow Tone,* and other jazz lovers' favorites. Among the numerous songs and instrumental numbers he enjoyed playing most were: *My Funny Valentine, Autumn Leaves, All Blues, Blue Train, and Black Orpheus.*

Garcia had a full repertoire comprised of a wide variety of music. Since he read music, he was able to play any kind of music on the harp.

Robert amazed audiences with his versatility on the harp, and he opened their minds to the instrument's many possibilities. After experiencing Garcia's performances, some listeners would walk up to him and say, "I've never heard the harp played that way," or "I've never heard anything other than classical music played on the harp before." Others would exclaim, "I love the music you played," or "I love how you played that harp!"

PHOTO GALLERY

Robert Garcia playing the harp at a family
reunion at Howard University in the early 1990s

Ron Gregg, Robert Garcia, and Ed Lanier, at a
gig in the Tampa Bay area in the early 1990s

Virginia and Robert at a restaurant in South Tampa circa 1997

Inside his home on Bonito Street, in Tampa, Garcia takes a moment from practicing to smile for his wife's camera.

In the late 1990s, and in what was for him by then a rare appearance on drums, Garcia performs at an engagement on New Year's Eve.

Apparently amused and not quite ready to pose are Robert Garcia, drummer-singer Turk Nelson (Center) and bassist William "B" Bennett

**In the summer of 2000, Garcia performs
in a nightclub in St. Louis, Missouri**

Garcia smiling for the camera after a performance in Lakeland, Florida

Virginia and Robert pose for the camera after his harp performance at the Tampa Bay Performing Arts Center, in the late 1990s

Along with the steady playing Robert did in secular venues, he reserved some time to play in church. He played drums one Sunday each month at the First Baptist Church of College Hill, and he played harp two Sundays a month at Allen Temple A.M.E., his home church in Tampa. He arranged music for church programs, weddings, receptions and other occasions. Additionally he ministered to senior citizens by playing harp music in nursing homes and in independent retirement facilities.

He also provided music clinics for school children. Teachers at various Florida schools learned of Robert's skill as a harpist. They invited him to their schools to talk to the students and to show them how the harp is played. During his clinics at elementary and middle schools, Robert was very generous with his time.

*** *** ***

One of the highlights of Robert Garcia's later years was that he assisted in the planning, development, and production of the Fourth Annual International Jazz Hall of Fame Induction and Awards Ceremony. That event was presented to a huge, excited audience at the Ice Palace, in Tampa, on November 21, 1997. Robert and Virginia Garcia were honored to socialize with such luminaries as the saxophonist and University of Pittsburgh jazz studies director Nathan Davis, and his wife author Ursula Broschke Davis with whom they shared a table at the event; and pianist Horace Silver.

Throughout the 1990s, Robert Garcia was approached and hired by individuals and organizations to play harp in various venues. Also, he aggressively pursued harp engagements on his own and through entertainment agencies. Garcia was steadily employed as a harpist for the remainder of his life. His untimely death occurred on August 6, 2001. His passing affected his family, friends and fellow musicians, and others in all walks of life.

ROBERT M. GARCIA'S LEGACY

ROBERT M. GARCIA'S LEGACY

Robert Michael Garcia was a magnificent talent on the drums. He should always be remembered for that. However, he should also be remembered as the wonderful harpist that he became through his giftedness, study, and diligence. His joy during the latter part of his life, in terms of a musical instrument, was the grand harp. Garcia indicated to those who knew him well that playing harp music helped him to be peaceful and calm in what was becoming an increasingly troubled world. Playing harp also allowed him to please and help a great many people. It gained him entry into a wide variety of venues and socially diverse events, which he thoroughly enjoyed.

Robert left a shining legacy for those who knew and loved him and to those who did not know him personally but will know his story now through this book. They will further know his story through the musicians who knew him and who continue to spread the good word about him. Some of those musicians have helped this book's author pass on Robert Garcia's legacy by sharing their thoughts about him as a man and as a musician. Those thoughts, which provide interesting information not mentioned elsewhere in this book, appear in the musicians' comments shown on the following pages.

QUOTES FROM FELLOW MUSICIANS

*** *** ***

Robert was one of the nicest guys I ever met. He always looked out for his band as far as eating and payment were concerned.

As a musician, he had one of the best techniques. He was versatile. He went from drums to harp. He was a phenomenal musician. He saw areas in music that hadn't been explored by other musicians, and he explored them to the max.

— Henry Ashwood, Saxophonist
St. Petersburg, Florida

*** *** ***

Robert was an institution of musical knowledge. . . . I was amazed to see that he went to Berklee as a drummer and came back [to Tampa] playing vibes and the harp. When the Montereys and I separated due to the increasing cost of travel, I stayed in contact with various friends in the Tampa area. . . . I found out that Robert was providing private music lessons in the Tampa area.

— Whitman Able, Guitarist
Memphis, Tennessee

Bobby was always upbeat. He was consistent, always the same. And Bobby was amazing with his creativity. The fact that he [once] built a harp was very impressive.

— Rose Bilal, Jazz Singer
Tampa, Florida

*** *** ***

Robert was great and humble, two traits that don't usually happen in the same person. He never boasted about his accomplishments or talents, but they became evident to all when he played … his harp or his drums. He was the same with everyone, no pretenses, just genuine Robert, a God fearing man, who often spoke of God and the woman whom he was blessed to share his life with.

The first time I saw him perform on his harp, I was pleasantly surprised! I immediately went to re-introduce myself to him. There was no need to. He remembered me. Up to that point I had only known him as a percussionist. He invited me to play numerous times with him and other local jazz musicians. I'd always ask when we were going to rehearse, and he would say: "We're just going to have fun, just bring your fake book." And he was right! We had so much fun! Those type gigs helped me as a player to be spontaneous and just enjoy the musical moments. And now, when I have a gig, I just have fun.

— Normita Rodriquez Jeffery,
Keyboardist Ladyfingers
Tampa, Florida

*** *** ***

We go back a long way. I always had fun around Bobby. I was always happy to see him. I remember when he met his wife, Virginia. It was back in 1990. He brought her to a gig we were doing during the Christmas Holidays. We were playing downtown at the *Barnett Building, on the 42nd floor. That was a good gig. We had fun.

— Shaheed Darby, Trumpet Player
St. Petersburg, Florida

*** *** ***

Robert was a warm spirit and a great friend, I've known him since 1977, and he was a member of the first band I ever led. We had Karl Goodspeed on piano, Barb Clary on vocals, I played bass, and Robert was on the drums. He made the band swing hard and sound full with his unique style of drumming. Robert lived down the street from me during this time and didn't have a car, so I'd run by his mother's house and pick him up for the gig, somehow managing to fit his drums and my bass in the back of my little Ford! Those were fun times.

— Michael Ross, Bassist
Tampa, Florida

---

*   Now the Bank of America Building

*** *** ***

Robert Garcia: a man of few words but with so much to say, verbally and musically.

> — Ed Lanier, Bassist
> New Jersey; Tallahassee and
> Lakeland, Florida

*** *** ***

Robert was a good friend. He was a good person and a family man. He was always building something, changing things on his house. I respected him for those things. And I respected him when he changed instruments. He stuck with the harp until he got it, and he kept it going.

> — William "B" Bennett, Bassist
> Tampa, Florida

*** *** ***

When I first knew of Robert Garcia, he was a percussionist and so was I, so our paths didn't cross very often. I first worked with him when he started playing the harp as his primary instrument and he asked me to work on a gig with him. We played the opening of an exhibit of Jonathan Green's paintings at the African-American Art Museum in Tampa. I was amazed how Robert used the harp as an instrument for playing jazz and did it so well. His expectations of those who played in his group were for them to be quality musicians also. I remember him mostly as a jazz musician, but he could play blues, funk, Latin— Robert Garcia could play it all.

The more I worked with Robert, the more I realized the kind of person he was. He was very smart and quite clever. Most of all I found him to be thoughtful. He would always put others before himself. We often shared our thoughts about life and relationships and he would not hesitate to help someone, perhaps to become a better person or a better musician. His love for his family was very evident and touching.

— Ron Gregg, Drummer
St. Petersburg, Florida

*** *** ***

I only knew Robert a very short time. Yet time is relative and in that short time I came to know him as a very genuine person, with a lot of God's light shining through him. We worked together as musicians, yet I found him to be all about caring, helping others and sharing his ideals and light and smile! He really walked the walk. His spirit lifted a room up and brought out the best in those around him. Family was important to him and I will always consider him a brother.

The first time we met and performed together was for a Christmas party and I thought I was meeting a blues harp player! I walked in and he was at the top of this beautiful staircase with his beautiful harp all set up, smiling and calling out to me, "Linda, I'm Robert". We played absolutely in sync from the first song, and it felt like we had been playing together for years. After a bit of classical flute and harp and Christmas carols, we broke into some amazing jazz tunes and it was a great joy. People that evening thought we had been working together for twenty years; which is funny because I had been looking for a harpist that long! We had some lofty plans musically and in the few short months working together, we played some great music.

— Linda Nash, Flutist
Clearwater, Florida

*** *** ***

When I first had the opportunity to work with Robert Garcia, I was a young twenty year-old R&B musician. I'd heard a lot about Robert in the weeks before we played the job, about him being a great jazz drummer. We performed with Johnny Killen, a singer in the mode of James Brown. The job was a weekend in Jacksonville, Florida.

That weekend in Jacksonville, playing with Robert was the first time that I played with a true jazz musician. Robert had so much finesse with the drums, and yet he played with so much power! I had played with powerful drummers before, but no one as powerful as Robert. And I had never played with a drummer who was as musical as Robert. He approached the drums as an instrument that played melodies as well as rhythm.

Robert was not only a great musician but also a great person. He had a positive attitude toward life, which was also reflected in his playing. I remember him helping other musicians load their equipment after he finished with his. I also remember him telling me about how good marriage was for him.

— Vincent Sims, Guitarist
Tampa, Florida

*** *** ***

Yes indeed, Bobby and I went a ways back. I can remember meeting Rigoberto's son at the R&A Sundries on 22nd Street and Chipco Street. The owner of the Sundries was an old Cuban guy (who was Spanish!!!), who was friends with a lot of Afro- Cuban American families in and out of the Belmont Heights neighborhood, where his store was located. It had to be the late '50s when I met the shy little Robert.

I was reacquainted with Bobby some years later, when I was in high school and he was playing snare drum and tympani drums at a local junior high school. He was still quiet as a teen but he was intensely engrossed in music, melodic and percussive. Then there were the times when Robert was studying (Berklee, USF, and FAMU) and playing Jazz locally and traveling. I made quite a few avant-garde gigs with Bobby.

Later in Bob's life, I noticed his attachment to the lyre and harp. He was so intensely enamored of the harp; until he borrowed some of my wood craft tools, bought more tools and began to make his own harps from raw material. I thought that was very admirable for an artist or musician to endeavor.

Robert Garcia will always be in my heart and thoughts as a friend and musical compatriot. I miss the kindred spirit of the man.

I often think of a trip I took along with Virginia and Robert, such a wonderful trip and a beautiful memory of Robert -- happy and at peace with himself.

— Chico Arenas, Trombonist
Tampa, Florida

Robert Garcia's Favorite Poems from Books Written by His Wife, Virginia Garcia

Robert Garcia attended many of the poetry readings that Virginia performed in Tampa and elsewhere in the Bay area. He played harp music while she read her poems to very appreciative audiences in books stores such as Three Birds Book Store, in Ybor City; Wilhite Collectibles Bookstore in Clearwater; Barnes and Noble, in Tampa; and Books for Thought, in Tampa. He also accompanied her readings at some of the Hillsborough County Libraries; area churches; museums, and private art galleries. Of the several published collections from which Virginia read her poems, Robert liked those from *The Love Zone* best. And he was happy to hear his friend, Donald Latson, relate the following story regarding poems from *The Love Zone*.

When Donald first began pursuing the busy career woman he later married, he had a hard time reaching her by phone and had to leave voice mail messages for her. Soon he started reading a poem from *The Love Zone* as his voice mail message to her. Donald was convinced that it was those poems that actually helped him win his wife Joyce's heart. Robert was delighted to hear that story and proud that Virginia was the author of the poems that brought two of his friends closer together and helped lead them to the altar.

Another of Virginia's poetry books that Robert particularly enjoyed was *The Blackberry Sketchbook,* a collection of humorous and serious prose poems about Black Culture. Some of Robert's favorite poems from the above mentioned books appear on the next several pages.

Poems from THE LOVE ZONE

A LOVE FOR ALL SEASONS

In winter your love is
a fluffy blanket keeping
me warm on cold nights
and frosty mornings.
In spring it's a light-weight
jacket protecting me from
chafing winds and penetrating
showers.
It's the sun's sensual touch or
a balmy breeze embracing me.
Your love in summer is a
cool ocean breeze alleviating
sweltering heat.
In autumn, your love is a wrap
about my shoulders on crisp
mornings and chilly evenings.
Your love envelopes me during all
the seasons, and it's nurtured me
during the seasons of my life.
Need I offer other reasons
why having you in my life is
so right?

LOVE POWER

1

Your love is solar power –
energizing as it generates
warmth in me and charges
me to achieve what I had
thought was impossible.

#2

Your love is stellar power -
illuminating me, inspiring me
to become a star.

NO OTHER LOVE

There is no other
who can see your
joy, your pain ...
longing, contentment
in turn as well as I.

There is no other
who can look beyond
your faults and see
your need –
accept you completely
as I have accepted you.

And there is no other
who can love me
as well as you have
loved me --
or for as long.

And that is why
for all this time
there has been
no other real love
for me ...
but you.

Poems from
THE BLACKBERRY SKETCHBOOK

* FOUR ARTISTS HANGIN' OUT IN YBOR CITY

A big, medium brown harpist from Tampa;
his shaven-head, dancer-from-New York friend;
a café con leche Atlanta born poet;
and a DC- bred writer with cinnamon skin
were hangin' out in Tampa's Ybor City
one breezy spring night in June.

They started in a crowded art gallery
Listenin' to a brother read his poems,
and they lifted him up with solid applause
as he read his Tampa songs.
They greeted him when the reading was done,
and then the four moved leisurely on.

After strolling along Ybor City streets –
passing shops, galleries, and boutiques
they stopped for a late night meal.
And at the same club, The Blues Ship,
they listened to some "down 'n' out" tunes.

Again they walked the City's streets
enjoying the seductive air -
feeling soft breezes, loving palm trees
laughing, joking, swapping stories,
talking about performing together one day
with a contract that would be fair.

A big, medium brown harpist from Tampa;
his shaven-head, dancer-from-New York friend;
a café con leche Atlanta born poet;
and a DC - bred writer with cinnamon skin –
four artists hangin' out in Ybor City
one breezy spring night in June.

THIS FAMILY

Bound by blood
struggle
pain
good times
love,
this family is
life blood
evidence of my history
my existence.

This family –
separated at times
by miles
beliefs
life styles –
is brought together again
by a need to feel connected;

brought together
by the bond
the love;

brought together again
brought together again …
brought together …
again.

THANKSGIVING

A woman is cooking and baking
for her family, who loves her
in return.

This brown ginger woman
wears well those lines of laughter,
worry, pain that time has engraved
on her forehead and at the corners of
her eyes and mouth.

She models with dignity the salt 'n' pepper
virgin hair that compliments her face.

Good smells floating from her
kitchen, traveling all through
the house, carry messages that
a feast is being prepared.

GOOD smells –
the turkey in its juices
candied yams
collard greens
creamy mashed potatoes
rich giblet gravy
piping hot rolls – all saying:
"Love is in this house."

Good smells floating from her
kitchen, traveling throughout
the house are saying, "A LOVE
feast is being prepared."

Watering mouths, smiles, contentment
are happening throughout this home and
responding, "We DO give thanks."

AFTERWORD

Traditionally the pedal harp has been regarded as an elite musical instrument, played more by delicate looking women than by men. Perhaps that is so because most people associate the grand harp with classical music. And many people's most immediate mental image of a harpist is a woman musician with small hands and slender fingers. It was amazing therefore for audiences to see musician Robert M. Garcia, a strapping middle-aged man, with large hands and thick fingers playing the grand harp.

The history of jazz includes five African American harpists: two women and three men. The first woman, jazz harpist Dorothy Ashby (1931 – 1986), recorded a number of albums in the 1950s. The other woman, jazz harpist Alice Coltrane (1937 - 2007), recorded essential albums in the late 1960s and early 1970s.

Notable among the men was harpist Robert M. Garcia (1950 – 2001). At the time of his death, there were only two other African American male harpists of note: Jeff Majors of Washington, DC, and Calvin Stokes of Cleveland, Ohio.

All of the African American harpists mentioned above studied and played various other instruments (xylophone, vibraphone, piano, organ, horns, etc.) before switching to the grand harp. But only one of them, Robert M. Garcia, switched from *drums* to harp.

AUTHOR'S NOTE

There is a street in Paris, France, called rue de la Harpe. The English translation is *street of the harp*, or Harp Street. Thinking of that street's name makes me smile because of my former marital and artistic connection to the late harpist Robert M. Garcia.

Early in the year 2000, Robert and I talked about and looked forward to traveling to Paris together the next year. He knew that my first novel, Forbidden Circles (the first edition), which he helped me promote, was set in Paris. I believe he wanted to see for himself some of the monuments and other places in Paris that

I had described in my book. And we both wanted to visit some concert halls and jazz venues there. But sadly due to his untimely passing in August 2001, we were not able to fulfill our plan to travel to Paris together.

Several years after Robert passed, I traveled to France alone and I felt that his spirit was in Paris with me. It was during the planning of a subsequent trip to Paris that I discovered the existence of the rue de la Harpe. My travel agent reserved a room for me in a hotel on that street. Discovering the existence of the rue de la Harpe was, for me, a spiritual experience. I was compelled therefore to get to know the street through research as well as through the soles of my feet.

The rue de la Harpe is located in the heart of the Latin Quarter. It is said that the name came from a standard of King David playing a harp. Centuries ago, the rue de la Harpe was known as the "heart of the students," or the main street that had student housing, small food shops, and workshops. Today it is a vibrant street of restaurants, cafés, a hotel, an Internet café, souvenir shops, a sorbet parlor, and boutiques.

I found the rue de la Harpe to be a pleasant place to stroll. It is full of life, with people laughing and chatting as they sit together and eat at outdoor café tables. The boutiques and souvenir shops on the street showcase affordable items in their windows. In nice weather, musicians and singers compete for the corner of the rue de la Harpe. People who appreciate good music sometimes gather to watch performances there.

On different days, I witnessed different musicians playing outside my hotel, near the front door. One day, I saw an olive-hued musician playing the violin. On another day, a fair-skinned musician was playing the accordion. And on still another day, I saw a guitarist playing music in front of the hotel, on the street named for the instrument played by King David and other special musicians, including harpist Robert M. Garcia.

Before I left Paris, I photographed the rue de la Harpe sign. Although I do not need a photo of a Paris street sign to remind me of Robert and his talent as a harpist, my having an image of the sign in my possession is nice. It reminds me that Robert was planning for us to visit Paris together; and that my visits there were tributes to him and to the two of us. The photo of the street sign, my in-person viewing of the sign and the street itself are mementos I've associated with my knowledge of Robert's talent and skill as a musician and my wonderful memories of our connection in the arts, and the extraordinary life we shared together.

****** ******* *******

I welcome emails from readers who have enjoyed or in any way benefited from the information published in *FROM DRUMS TO HARP: the Story of Drummer and Harpist Robert M. Garcia*. My email address is: jazzeight3@aol.com.

Anyone with a request concerning events or appearances may email it to me. For more information, please visit my website, **www.veegarcia.com**. Thank you for your interest in FROM DRUMS TO HARP.

Vee Williams Garcia

APPENDIX I

Instruments Robert Garcia Played Professionally

Kinds of Duos in Which He Played

Various Ensembles in Which He Played

Video Tape Demos

CD Demos

INSTRUMENTS ROBERT GARCIA PLAYED PROFESSIONALLY

Conga drums

Xylophone

Vibraphone

Drum set

Grand harp

DUOS IN WHICH
ROBERT GARCIA PLAYED

Grand harp and upright bass

Harp and flute

Harp and violin

Harp and cello

Harp and voice

Harp and piano

ENSEMBLES

TRIOS:

Grand harp, upright bass, and drums

Harp, violin, cello

Harp, guitar, trombone

Harp, drums, guitar

OTHER SMALL GROUPS:

Grand harp, violin, viola, cello

Harp, bass, drums, trumpet

Harp, bass, drums, saxophone

Harp, bass guitar, drums

Harp, bass, drums, trumpet, saxophone

VIDEO TAPE DEMO

Jazz Video (untitled)

Partial list of Tunes

In a Mellow Tone
Black Orpheus
All of Me
Killer Joe
When Sunny Gets Blue

Musicians:

Robert Garcia (harp)
Ron Gregg (drum set)
William Bennett (upright bass)

———

CD DEMO

Jazz/ Pop CD:

"Beautiful Music of the Flute & Harp"

Tunes:

Song for My Father
Yesterday
God Bless the Child
Killer Joe

Musicians:

Robert Garcia (harp)
Linda Nash (flute)

---

*   Early in 2001, Robert M. Garcia made plans to produce a commercial CD the next year with his trio, Robert Garcia and Friends. However he became ill and passed away in August 2001, several months before he was able to implement those plans.

APPENDIX II

General Performance Venues

Some Specific Venues Where
Robert Garcia Played Drums and Harp

Cities Where Garcia Played Drums and Harp

GENERAL VENUES WHERE ROBERT GARCIA PLAYED MUSIC

Performing Arts Centers
Convention Centers
Churches
Sorority/Fraternity Houses
Private Homes
Hospitals
Retirement Centers
Military Installations
Book Stores, Libraries
Museums
Grade Schools
Community Colleges
Universities
Hotels, Country Clubs
Nightclubs, Restaurants
Concert Halls, Theaters
Open-air Jazz Festivals

SOME SPECIFIC VENUES IN TAMPA-ST. PETERSBURG WHERE GARCIA PLAYED DRUMS AND THE HARP

*Museum of African American Art, Tampa
Alpha Kappa Alpha House, Tampa
Tampa Bay Performing Arts Center
Vinoy Renaissance Hotel, St. Petersburg
Don Cesar Hotel, St. Petersburg
Marriott Airport Hotel, Tampa International Airport
Marriott Hotel Downtown, Tampa
Hampton House of Jazz, Tampa
The Garden Club, St. Petersburg
The University of South Florida Art Museum, Tampa
Hunters Green Country Club, Tampa
Tampa Palms Country Club
First Baptist Church of College Hill
Allen Temple A.M.E. Church
Hillsborough Community College, Ybor City Campus, Tampa
Ybor City Jazz Festivals, Tampa
Brad Cooper Gallery, Ybor City, Tampa
Hilton Hotel
Crown Colony Hotel
Hyatt Hotel, downtown Tampa
Wyndham Hotel
The Florida Aquarium
Borders Books & Music, South Tampa
Saffron's Restaurant, St. Petersburg
Valencia Gardens Restaurant, Tampa
Tampa Convention Center

---

*   On many occasions, Garcia played at the Museum of African American
       Art, in Tampa, from 1992 until it closed in 1996.

SOME OF THE CITIES WHERE
GARCIA PLAYED MUSIC

*Inside Florida

Brooksville
Clearwater
Daytona Beach
Dunedin
Ft. Pierce
Gainesville
Jacksonville
Lakeland
Land O-Lakes
Miami
Orlando
Sarasota
Spring Hill
Tallahassee
Tampa/St. Petersburg
West Palm Beach

**Outside Florida

Boston, Massachusetts
Chicago, Illinois
Hampton, Virginia
Knoxville, Tennessee
New Orleans, Louisiana
St. Louis, Missouri
Washington, D.C.

---

* At the time of his death, in August 2001, Robert Garcia's calendar was filled for the remainder of the year plus eight months into 2002 with engagements for which he had contracted to play throughout Florida and in **Detroit, Michigan.

APPENDIX III

Some of the Social and Religious Organizations for Which
Robert Garcia Played Harp

Volunteer Services Robert Garcia Provided

Awards, Recognition, Tributes

SOME OF THE SOCIAL AND RELIGIOUS ORGANIZATIONS FOR WHICH ROBERT PLAYED THE HARP

The Links
Alpha Kappa Alpha Sorority
Delta Sigma Theta Sorority
Kappa Alpha Psi Fraternity
Saturday's Children
Tampa Organization of Black Affairs (TOBA)
Sun Coast Hospital Foundation, Inc.

AME Churches
AME Zion Churches
United Methodist Churches
Baptist Churches
Catholic Churches
Jewish Synagogues

---

*   Sometimes Robert sang while he played hymns, anthems, and spirituals. He had a full, resonant bass voice.

VOLUNTEER SERVICES THAT ROBERT GARCIA PROVIDED

Drum and Harp Clinics in Schools

Hillsborough County Schools
Pinellas County Schools
Other county school districts in Florida

Drum or Harp Performances in Church Services

<u>In Tampa</u>:

Our Lady of Perpetual Help Catholic Church
Sacred Heart Catholic Church
St. Peter Claver Catholic Church
Allen Temple A.M.E. Church
First Baptist Church of College Hill
River Grove United Methodist Church
Keeney United Methodist Church

<u>In other Florida Cities</u>:

Orlando,
West Palm Beach,
Jacksonville,
Tallahassee,
Gainesville

<u>Cities Outside Florida</u>:

Washington, DC
Chicago, Illinois

Private Drum Instructions for Children

One to one lessons
Group lessons

Harp Music for Hospital Patients

St. Joseph's Hospital, Tampa, Florida
Tampa General Hospital,
University Community Hospital, Tampa, Florida

AWARDS AND SPECIAL RECOGNITION
ROBERT GARCIA RECEIVED

2001: Letter of Acceptance (for future work at Disney World) from Universal Studios, Orlando.

1998: Played harp at the home of Hillsborough Community College President Gwendolyn Stephenson (Christmas Party).

1997: Assisted in the planning, research, development, and production of The Fourth Annual International Jazz Hall of Fame Induction and Awards Ceremony, held at the *Ice Palace in downtown Tampa, Florida, November 20-21, 1997.

1995: Award from the Florida Endowment Fund for services rendered to the Museum of African American Art and to various McKnight Fellowship events.

1990s: Certificates of Appreciation from many elementary and secondary schools for music clinics provided and performances rendered.

1986: Appreciation Award: Service to Gwen's School of Music, in Tampa, Florida.

---

*   Now known as the St. Petersburg Times Forum

POSTHUMUS TRIBUTES

"Robert Garcia and His Music"— a tribute presented by the Hampton House of Jazz; Tampa, Florida, September 23, 2001.

"Resolution for Brother Robert Garcia" from the Music Department of Allen Temple A.M.E. Church; Tampa, Florida, August 11, 2001.

"Resolution" from the Senior Adult Choir, First Baptist Church of College Hill; Tampa, Florida, August 11, 2001.

Masses held in Robert M. Garcia's honor by Our Lady of Perpetual Help Catholic Church; Tampa, Florida, September 16, 2001; May 26, 2002; August 18, 2002 and annually in August since 2002.

ABOUT THE AUTHOR

Vee Williams Garcia was born and reared in Washington, DC. She was educated in public schools and at the University of the District of Columbia; where she majored in English. Garcia completed additional studies in English and Literature at the University of South Florida, in Tampa.

From 1994 – '96, Vee Garcia taught poetry at the East Tampa Horizon School, in Tampa, Florida. During the next ten years, she wrote and had poetry, feature articles, short stories, and books published.

Garcia has three published novels to her credit. They are: *Whatever It Takes, Forbidden Circles,* and *The Jazz Flower.*

From Drums to Harp: the Story of Drummer and Harpist Robert M. Garcia is Vee Williams Garcia's first book of non-fiction.

Vee Garcia resides in the United States of America, and divides her time between Florida, Washington, DC, and Maryland. She is working on her next book. For further information, please visit **www.veegarcia.com.**

NOTES

NOTES

NOTES

NOTES

Manufactured By: RR Donnelley
                     Breinigsville, PA USA
                     October, 2010